The Trip

He followed that up with, "Papa, you should see how big her top is and she has a fantastic bottom, too." At that point I wanted to ask him if she was pretty or not, but I was afraid he hadn't looked that high up yet!

Nine days before his 70th birthday, a grandfather gets the crazy idea that he can take his five adolescent grandsons on a 2-day trip to Michigan's Upper Peninsula, and everything will be okay. His wife and the boy's mothers know better, but he is not deterred.

All goes well, till the fateful meeting with Ms. Bikini; then, all bets are off. Before The Trip is over, Grandpa and the boys learn more about themselves than they

ever imagined in just two days:
Not all of it good.

Learn how they not only survived
The Trip but made memories that
will last their entire lifetimes and
created bonds of love that will
never be broken.

Dedication

This book is dedicated to the Fab Five, our fantastic grandsons, who for a short moment in time transported me back to the golden days of my own adolescence.

Thank you, Casey "Silk" Marcum—Joe "Joey D" Dell'Anno 1V—Joshua "Hoops" Marcum— Kyle "Mr. Homerun" Minder— and Justin "Personality Plus" Marcum... you boys gave your ol' grandfather memories that will warm his heart forever.

My hope is that you will keep "The Trip" forever. There will surely be days, later on in your lives, when you may wonder why you were even born. Life is not perfect but is constantly changing and is often a challenge that has to be met head on.

When those days come, read our story once more and remember that tough times don't last, but tough people always do. Think back to those days when everything was possible and realize, once more, that it still is.

Remember, always, the love that Grandma Lee and Papa hold deep in their hearts for each of you; and always be true to yourself; your family; your friends; and to God.

Casey

Our 16-year-old grandson, Casey, was coming to visit us from his home in Corpus Christi, Texas. It would be the 2nd straight year he came to Michigan, and last year had been unbelievable.

When Grandma Lee and I picked him up from the airport, as we started our trip up I-94, we saw the Blue Angels, who were putting on a show.

We pulled off to the side of the expressway and watched these fabulous flyboys entertain the huge crowd with their aerial acrobatics for about 20 minutes before continuing to our home in Pinckney.

Of course, I told him his grandpa had arranged the show especially for him. With our annual, Grandma's Picnic at Portage Yacht Club, his stay just seemed to get better each day he was with us.

Our challenge was to make his 2 week stay with us even better this year. It seemed an impossible task for his Grandma and me, but we looked forward to giving it our best shot.

When he was here last year, we had hoped to take him across the Mackinaw Bridge to the beautiful Upper Peninsula of our state. It didn't work out though, so I was determined to do it this year.

Casey has four cousins close to his age, who share his love of sports, here in Michigan. They are all good students, too, and each one is a really good kid. The oldest is Joey, age 14, followed by Joshua, age 13, and Justin and Kyle, both age 12.

I approached my wife a few days after Casey had been here and told her I would like to take the five boys to Mackinaw Island and several other places we knew that we were sure they would all enjoy. I wanted it to be a boy's only trip—no girls allowed...not even her.

We would stay at our favorite motel in St Ignes. It has a lovely beach with a truly beautiful view of the Island and the surrounding area.

Grandma Lee thought it was a fantastic idea but worried if a soon to be 70-year-old, could handle five young men their ages for two whole days. I assured her I was up to the task.

We contacted all the mothers and got okays from all but Kyle's mom. Kyle had to attend a sports camp, so he would not be able to go. We were all disappointed but would make the best of it without him.

Things changed a few days before we left when Kyle's mom, Tammy, gave him the choice of baseball camp or the trip. He replied, "Mom, are you kidding? I want to go with my cousins!"

Now things were absolutely perfect! We would leave by 8 Tuesday morning and come home Thursday afternoon.

I began preparing food for us two days before we were to leave. The kids love chocolate chip pancakes, so I made 20 for our 2nd day in St. Ignes and covered them tightly with cling wrap to keep them fresh.

The motel we were staying at had a tiny refrigerator and a small microwave, so I planned our menu with the microwave in mind.

It took several hours both days till I had all we needed to eat, already prepared. We would only have to stop for breakfast Sunday morning, and we would eat like kings while we were there... well, almost, anyway.

Four of the boys would spend the night before we left with their grandmother and me, while

Casey would meet us about 3 hours away in Gaylord. He had left a day earlier with his uncle Doug and his son Brenden. They were going to a cottage my son and his wife had recently purchased and in addition to having a good time on the lake the cottage sat on, they were going to replace a wall inside the cottage.

Casey totally loves spending time with his uncle Doug and Brenden and the feeling is mutual. They always seem to have a great time together doing fun and exciting things like water skiing and fishing, or just hanging out together.

I wanted to see just what the new generation of men in our family was growing into, so I decided to leave a lot of grandpa at home and just relax with the boys, who were all at that special age when their lives change, forever.

It is such an awkward time for boys but, perhaps, the most joyful they will ever experience. I was not going to be just a fly on the wall though but, also, a participant in their conversations, at least to a small degree.

I planned on letting them say in front of me what they would surely say when my back was turned. Words like condoms and sex; even hot chicks!

Whatever they decided to talk about, Grandpa was in for it. I was going to have fun with these fantastic grandsons of ours!

The four of them were all at our house by 6, Monday evening. Each boy's spirit was at an all-time high just thinking of their coming adventure with each other and their Papa. We all went to bed early—quite a change for the boys.

Tuesday, Grandma Lee and I got up at 5 am. We showered, and then I started breakfast for 4 starving boys. They ate four or more chocolate chip pancakes each, smothered in syrup, and gobbled down over a pound of turkey bacon along with a couple of juice pouches to wash it all down with. Man, that is a breakfast supreme!

After eating, we carried our bags out to Grandma Lee's van, and then we loaded the big cooler full of food and 8 large containers of juice pouches for our fantastic journey. Grandma Lee got four big hugs and lots of kisses from her handsome grandsons, as well as a couple from me, too....She crossed her fingers and wished me luck. Not much later I would surely need it!

We pulled out of our driveway at 8:02am —not bad I thought only 2 minutes behind schedule and we had a full tank of gas.

Mackinaw, here we come!

On the Road Again

Right from the start, the four boys were laughing and talking animatedly, even as we backed out of the driveway. It was, almost, as if they knew how memorable this trip was going to be. But at that moment, none of us really knew what was to come….I may have pulled that van right back into our garage if I did.

We had to put the big cooler in the back seat, sitting perpendicular, to make room for all our passengers. The two boys who would take the least space would have to sit on either side of the cooler.

Till we picked up Casey, only Justin had to sit there. Joey was in front with me, and Kyle and

Josh were in the seats behind us. Within 15 minutes we were on US 23, headed north.

In another 45 minutes, we would be passing by Flint, Michigan, once a powerhouse of manufacturing. We merge with I–75 a few miles before Flint and take it straight to the beautiful Mackinaw Bridge where we will cross into Michigan's, Upper Peninsula.

It was about 9 am when we drove through the Flint area, so the traffic was fairly heavy. We would have another 45 minutes before the traffic thinned out, and then we would enter the really peaceful and scenic drive north. The boys could have cared less, though. They were in 7th heaven just being together, and we were all anxious to get to

Gaylord, where we would take our last passenger on board.

About 25 miles from Gaylord, I called Doug. We decided to meet at a Burger King just off the expressway. We arrived only a couple of minutes before he did. After hugs and kisses for him and Brenden, Casey climbed into the van and we were off for the final hour or so before we came to the bridge. Casey took Josh's seat, and Josh moved to the back with his brother. Even with the cooler, Josh and Justin had ample room to relax.

The first thing Casey asked for was his phone. He had left it at our house when he left with his uncle. He later called, asking his grandmother to charge it for him. No young person today is complete without their smart phone. It is amazing to us old timers.

As Joshua handed Casey his phone, he told him he called his girlfriend in Texas the night before and talked to her. Then Josh related his conversation to Casey—none of it intended to give Casey a warm, fuzzy, feeling. Big mistake! You don't kid a teenager about his girlfriend.

Casey reacted normally, becoming instantly upset that his cousin would do something so outrageous. He kept demanding, "Did you really say that!" Josh just laughed and kept insisting that, yes, he really did.

The others were silent, watching and listening to this little drama, anxious to see what the outcome would be.

Before it got completely out of hand, I barked, "Joshua...did you really call Casey's girlfriend?" He admitted sheepishly that he didn't, and things settled down to a peaceful state, once more.

Actually, seeing all the Mackinaw Bridge's entire 26,376 feet span across the beautiful, blue, Straits of Mackinaw, is indeed a sight to behold. It was opened to the public on November 1st, 1957, and now requires a little annual upkeep. As we crossed today one lane was partially closed while workers were making repairs.

I had the boys call their mothers as they looked down the 154 feet to the Straits of Mackinaw, at the many different looking boats crossing under the bridge. There were freighters and other large ships as well as many pleasure boats of different colors and sizes; all, with plenty of room to navigate. It was a lovely sight to behold.

The joy in their voices was unmistakable as they each said, "Hi mom it's me! We're just crossing the bridge!" ...I felt proud that I was part of this.

We rode a little further to the toll booth and I paid our $4.00 toll and turned right into the lovely, little, city of St. Ignes. As we rode along the 2 lane road entering this small town, the boys were each taking the sights in. They looked in wonder across the water to the Island of Mackinaw and all the surrounding, breathtaking, scenery.

You could tell the character of this town by its shops and its people. It looked like the safest place in the world to be—that is, till one of the boys made a cat call at a pretty girl walking with her strong-looking, male companion. Immediately, I ordered, "No more of that!"

The guy looked like he wanted to come after us and, frankly, I wouldn't have blamed him.

At this point I wanted to impart some grandfatherly advice to our grandsons, but I knew Grandma Lee wouldn't have approved, so I resisted the temptation. I wanted to tell them to make sure there were girls and girls only that they complimented openly like that; **never** when they were walking with their boyfriends. Especially, monsters that looked like they could make you weep like a small child in front of your own mother!

As we drove slowly through town, we could see the many ferries taking hundreds of sightseers as well as a few natives over to the island. The wake the boats made shot 20 feet high. These boats were really fast, and they held lots of people and luggage as well as the ever present, bicycles.

Our young men were very happy they made this trip, as was I. We were all so excited by what lay ahead. If only we'd known then what we would later...but how could we?

It was a little after the noon hour and we were all hungry. We decided to check in to our motel before we headed to Mackinaw. I would heat the hamburger meat and the buns in the microwave, and the kids could decorate them as each wanted. That, and some chips & juice pouches, and we were ready for the day.

The motel clerk was extra nice; especially, to a lone man with five teenage boys. She didn't even charge us extra for the roll-away bed we would need. She also gave us a room with a wonderful view. Almost as importantly, it was one which I could see the adjacent, glass enclosed, pool house from the window of our room to keep track of my five teenage charges.

After eating, we climbed into the van and drove the two miles back to the boat ferry. We had three to choose from. The largest carrier is Arnold Lines; then

Shepler's; and then Star. We chose Shepler's; the first we came to.

My wife and I had not been here in several years so I was a little surprised when it cost $24 for each of us, except my two twelve year olds, who were only $12 each; about what I thought the tickets would cost for those older than 12 , also.

But, what the heck; the price of wonderful memories, sometimes, cost more than you think they will...I would really learn this later on.

We had a 30 minute wait till the next ferry ran. It was a beautiful sunny day with a perfect temperature of 71 degrees, so we didn't mind the wait. The boys all walked over to the end of the dock, watching the waves lap against it, 12 feet below. I snapped some pictures and before we knew it, we were loading.

We headed for the top deck. As soon as we were all seated, the captain maneuvered the 65-foot, Felicity, perfectly, away from the dock for the 15 minute ride, across the six mile expanse of blue water to Mackinaw Island.

The three older boys sat together, and I sat with Kyle and Justin. When the boat was a couple of miles away we could see the Grand Hotel, sitting high, on the side of the hilly terrain that is Mackinaw. It is a breathtaking sight to behold.

Fort Mackinaw was also clearly visible, as well as many other larger buildings, including our Governor's summer home. The flag was at half mast, indicating that he was not in residence, today.

Our Captain docked our boat without a hitch. Within minutes, we were on the dock walking the 50 feet to the city streets.

Horse Poop and Fudge

The first thing you notice is the smell; intriguing scents of horse poop and fudge. Where else in the world does it smell like this, I ask you....No where! This smell is totally unique...Believe me!

Since the only motorized vehicles on Mackinaw are the ambulances, which are rarely ever seen, and since there are lots of horse drawn carriages, as well as many individual horseback riders — there is always plenty of horse poop around. Even with the constant clean-up by the poop patrol.

There are plenty of fudge shops, too. They create some of the best tasting fudge in the entire world! It is almost a standoff between the wonderful smelling chocolates, and the not so good smelling, horse poop. Being the optimist I am; I think the chocolates, win.... But not by much!

My boys all had such excited looks on their faces. They were full of joy. They were laughing and talking a mile a minute! It was wonderful for me to witness myself, so many years earlier. I couldn't have been happier as I led them past the quaint and unique shops of this amazing island.

Our destination was the Grand Hotel, but we were not in a hurry to get there. We walked in unison with our fellow travelers, of which, there were many.
Laughing, and just being a buddy to them, I had them follow me. After all, I had been here before;

and besides —I was definitely the oldest!

As we walked up the increasingly steep sidewalk toward our destination, I directed them past a street that led to the left of us and not so much upward. After a block or two of extreme cardio workout, even a person with such a horrible sense of direction as I, could tell we should have taken the street we just passed. We turned around and walked back down the hill. Much easier going downhill and we didn't have to go very far, either.

As you walk up the steep grade toward the Grand Hotel and actually see it, up close, for the first time; it is simply a breathtaking sight! Such grace and tradition, built on this tiny island with only 600 year-round residents.

Not a hard, ugly, brick, to be seen anywhere on this fabulous structure. What a vision its creator had! It has the longest front porch; 660 feet, of any hotel in the world!

Its front porch has 260 planting boxes filled with more than 5200 Geraniums! Such beautiful flowers! They look so regal on this incredibly long and spacious structure. All the hotels guests, as well as all of its visitors, get to sit on this beautiful porch and enjoy a view so stunning—that it's equal, few will ever witness. In addition, they are served by the most courteous staff you could imagine.

We are here only two weeks before the 125th anniversary of this magnificent hotel. It opened on July 10th, 1887. There will certainly be a "Grand Celebration" this July 10th by the folks on Mackinaw, as well as many other guests and celebrities. And deservedly so!

My five handsome boys were seeing this for the first time; and they were seeing it with me. How much better can life get!

I had no trouble, at all, keeping up with them as we walked higher and higher up the steep sidewalk. There was even a spring in my step. Not bad for a man nearly 70, I thought. I was a very happy granddad, indeed! The smile on my face, as well as the gleam in my eyes, said it all.

The spring in my step was nothing compared to the five of them, though. They laughed with each other, and the sound of their voices. so carefree; it was hard for me to believe that I once thought the thoughts they were thinking and had their boundless energy and strong legs.

I was suddenly in state of "Aw Shit" I can't believe I was that young once upon a time! (I put this in for our nine-year granddaughter, Cassie. When we're out of Grandma Lee's ear–shot, we think of all the different ways to say, "aw shit" and all the different emphasis it can be said with. Then we laugh like crazy for being so naughty— hoping, Grandma Lee won't catch us!)

This was, definitely, a very sentimental, "aw shit" moment for me.

As we finally arrive at the top, where the ground levels off and we are only a few feet away from the hotel — we are directed inside to purchase "visitors passes" in order to go any farther. When my wife and I first came to this island many years ago; that wasn't the case. You could take a private tour, without charge.

That's changed now, and it cost me $50 for the six of us. To see this fabulous hotel, though, is nearly priceless.

Joey was wearing a tank-top which is a no-no. We had a short wait, till he was presented with a monogrammed, navy-blue, blazer to wear. It looked great on him, and this kid was more than happy to be the only one of us dressed to the nines.

Upon entering this magnificent place you are treated to such a huge expanse of lush, multi-colored carpeting in eye-catching greens, as well as other vibrant colors...along with such a spaciousness interior that's decorated so uniquely, it is simply hard for the brain to comprehend. Such a glorious display of vivid colors that all look so great together!

It gives me a feeling of pure joy and relaxation. Looking at my surroundings inside and then, looking out the huge windows to see the magnificent view of the water; the Mackinaw Bridge; and both cities of Mackinaw and St. Ignes. It boggles your mind!

Folks, this is really special! Grandma Lee would be so very proud, right now. I know she wishes she was here with us.

The boys and I enjoyed a leisurely tour of all the shops; took some pictures; then went outside where we headed down some steep stairs to the huge and lush, garden grounds. More importantly, to the swimming pool where we hoped to be treated to some other magnificent scenery...of the female type!

We were all, hugely, disappointed when we discovered that only hotel guests could get access to the pool; and the view.... This was really an Aw Shit moment!

Nothing sentimental about this Aw Shit though! Hey, I may be almost 70 but I'm not dead yet!

We spent the next hour taking in as much of the sights as we could; then, headed for a fudge shop. The walk down was much easier for me than the walk up. To the boys—they could care less!

On our way down we passed an elderly couple, both somewhat overweight. The poor guy was only a third up the grade and he looked as if he were climbing Mt. Everest. I felt sorry for him. Anguish and pain were written all over his face. They definitely should have taken a carriage instead of walking. We didn't hear any ambulance's sirens though, so I guess he made it okay.

Umm, Umm, Mackinaw Fudge

We chose a fudge shop where a young man was rolling fresh, hot, fudge on a 4-inch thick, marble, tabletop. It was about 3 feet square, allowing plenty of room for the candy maker to constantly roll and lift it with a tool called a spade or loafer. It looked like a miniature, wooden, boat paddle.

This keeps the sugar crystals from sticking together while a large batch of fudge is formed into about a two-inch-thick loaf. The smell inside this shop was absolutely scrumptious!

Unless you have been to a fudge shop like this, you can't even imagine the sensory sensation that greets your brain. An experience like this is exactly what your nose was created for, especially, when compared to the ever-present horse poop outside.

The deal of the day was three pounds for about twenty dollars. Casey got to choose one flavor then Joshua and Justin chose theirs, and finally Joey and Kyle chose theirs. But the boys all insisted on buying their own drinks. Hey, they are growing into men...

Leaving the shop, we checked the time our next ferry would leave for St. Ignes. Then we walked several blocks to the grounds just below Ft. Mackinaw to sample our candy.

I didn't think we'd ever get there. I was quickly getting tired....Really tired! These old legs had served me well today, but I couldn't wait to get back to the motel for some R & R. When we finally did arrive a fellow tourist gracefully gave up his seat on a bench, in a lovely shady area, so all my effervescent boys could sit together.

They eagerly shared their fudge so that each one could sample all the other different flavors. Justin saved a little of his and Josh's for their mother, just as he had promised her he'd do. The remainder of the fudge was devoured by the five of them.

Seeing the looks on their faces as they sat happily on that bench in this historic place...five young lives, each of whom I've been part of since their birth... gave me such an inner feeling of pure happiness. I thought, "Thank you Father."....My heart was full.

These boys of ours were having the time of their lives, and it was made so much better because they, truly, loved every minute they spent with each other. It was, definitely, a moment I would never forget. I guess you could say it was darn near perfect…. but with five boys their age—how much longer could it, possibly, stay that way?

After finishing the fudge, we walked to our boarding dock. Joshua offered to treat anyone to an ice cream cone. Only his best bud, Kyle, took him up on his offer. The other three were all sugared out.

They left the four of us and headed for the nearest ice cream shop. In just a few minutes they returned with double dippers.

After eating all he could, Kyle, asked if it was okay to walk over to the edge and drop what was left of his, into the water.

The second I said yes, Josh snatched it from his hand—but instead of walking the 15 feet to the edge and dropping it in like Kyle was going to do, he wound up and threw it like a baseball. We looked up to see the ice cream scoop, immediately, separate from the cone. We all thought, "No way is that going to make it."

I was sure it would fall on the walkway and make a sticky mess for people to have to walk through. Thankfully, it just made it over the edge and fell safely into the water below. A sea gull quickly started eating the cone, and the ice cream floated safely away as it quickly melted in the cool blue water of Lake Huron.

Our boat pulled into the dock just a few minutes later, and after its passengers unloaded, we got aboard. Kyle and Justin decided to stay below deck while the other boys and I went to the top deck to enjoy the wind whipping through our hair.

Before long, we were docking in St Ignes. As we left the boat and started back to the van, Justin told me how comfortable the seating was below, then, related that he and Kyle had each taken a short nap. I couldn't help but smile, thinking how like young boys that was. How many grownups could fall asleep that quickly....We should all be so lucky!

We boarded the van and headed for our motel room. The five boys were in a hurry to go swimming, and I was looking forward to a few minutes rest for first time today, since five that morning. It was now nearly five in the afternoon, so I had been on the go for 12 hours and the day was still young. This grandpa was quickly running out of energy.

The boys hurriedly changed into their swimming trunks and walked the few feet to the pool house. I waited a few minutes, then followed them to make sure they were not being too rowdy. The pool was quite large. Except for our five there was only a small girl in the pool. Her grandmother was sitting nearby reading a book and watching over her.

She was eight and cute as can be—and she could swim like a fish! She stayed totally to herself—not interacting at all with her fellow swimmers, but in fact, seemed rather oblivious of them as she swam the length of the long pool; then, back. A few hours later, I watched in awe as she swam the entire length of the pool underwater—not coming up a single time for a breath of air. It was nearly unbelievable that she could hold her breath that long.

The next day I learned from her grandmother that her name was Zoie. Her grandmother proudly told me that it was she who had taught her how to swim.

I had more important things to do though, so after watching the boys for a few minutes and cautioning them not to play too rough; I walked back to our room and carefully removed my sparkling wine glass from its packing. Next, I opened my favorite red wine and poured myself a glass of pure delight. I only packed one bottle, so this would yield two glasses of wine each day...if I only had the willpower to limit myself to 2 glasses today....Fat chance of that!

I walked onto our balcony and sat down, cradling my wine and sipping it, ever so slowly. The marvelous view...my wonderful wine...a soft breeze...being with my boys; I felt completely satisfied. This was the life!

After sitting outside for about 30 minutes, I walked back inside to get a refill and to start dinner. All

I had to do was get the chicken I had already made, along with the baked beans—put six ears of corn in the microwave, grab the dinner rolls, and presto; dinner was served!

Our table was next to the patio door and I could hear a lady a few rooms down, yelling something to her husband. When I looked out, I saw him standing at the water's edge looking toward a young man and woman further out in the lake.

MS Bikini

It was the woman that caught my eye. Even from 80 yards away, I could see she had quite a figure. I could see, also, that she was proud of it by the tiny bikini she was wearing. Little did I know at that moment what an important role she would play in the remainder of our stay.

It wasn't much later that I called the boys out of the pool to come eat. Little Zoie would have the pool all to herself, for a few minutes at least. They ate hurriedly like young men of their age do and headed back to the pool....this time they had company.

About 15 minutes later Joey, Josh, and Kyle, came back into the room, absolutely, bursting with excitement. They couldn't wait to tell me about Ms. Bikini.

Joey was the first to speak, saying that she was just 14 years old and that her name was, ------ -, which will not be mentioned on these pages. She will forever be known here as Ms. Bikini.

He followed that up with, "Papa, you should see how big her top is, and she has a fantastic bottom, too." At that point I wanted to ask him if she was pretty or not, but I was afraid he hadn't looked that high up yet!

Who could blame him! She had on one of the tiniest, black, string–bikini bottoms I had ever seen with a flowered top that was full to the brim. Most 20-year-old women would trade bodies with her without a second's hesitation.

She definitely had a figure that would stop a freight train, and she loved the attention it brought her. It was unbelievable to me that she was only 14...I was shocked. No one seeing this young woman would believe her age.

It was plain to see that Joey had forgotten all about seeing the Grand Hotel for the first time. Kyle and Joshua were just as excited as he was. If I had asked them what the Grand Hotel looked like at that moment they would probably have asked me what the heck I was talking about... what was a Grand Hotel, anyway!

Funny what Breasts and Butts do to the brain of us males at any age!

I asked Joey who the guy was. He answered that he was her cousin, and that they were here with their grandparents, who had taken them on vacation with them. He said the boy was their age and that he talked kinda' funny—that he thought the boy might be gay because he was wearing earrings in both ears. He added that it wouldn't matter to them if he were, they liked him anyway.

Hey, I guess that is what a boy wearing two earrings will make kids think these days. In my day one would have been more than enough to give that impression!

But, if you snooze, you lose. While they were giving me all these exciting details young Casey was making his move. From the looks of it he had already captured Ms. Bikini's heart as well as her complete attention. And he didn't even need his cowboy hat to impress.

I could see him with her and her cousin at the far end of the pool. It clearly looked as if they were enjoying themselves. Justin was with them, but it was apparent who she was interested in. Looks like my boy, Casey, had hit a home run this time at the plate.

For the rest of the evening, one or more of the kids would come to me, talking excitedly, while giving me an update on Ms. Bikini. They gave her a combined rating of 8. Boys will be boys! I must say I wondered…. Why only eight? Oh, yes it was her personality!

The pool closed at 10, so everyone went back to their rooms. The chatter among these guys was so filled with laughter. A lot of it, pure, devilish, laughter, if you know what I mean! Looks to me as if this lovely girl had just made this trip absolutely perfect! These boys were all crazy about her. That's what I thought at the time, anyway. Of course, time may very well prove me wrong about that.

I pulled the rollaway bed over near the sliding doors in the tiny space between the queen bed and the wall; unhooked it from the top and spread it out. This was almost exactly like the bed mom and dad had, that I slept in when I was their age. My three younger brothers slept in the larger bed in the room we shared.

Tonight, the three smallest boys got one queen bed while Casey and Joey got the other one, next to me. We had a big day planned for tomorrow, and we were all tired by now, so none of us had any problem falling asleep. That's what I thought at the time anyway…. Little did I know…..

I felt very good about our first day. It couldn't have been better. Even sleeping in this little bed, with the valley in the middle, wouldn't stop me from having sweet dreams, tonight.

Day 2

I awoke at my usual time of six am. I was surprised to see that Joey had left his bed and was sleeping on the floor between his bed and the dresser. I thought his back must be hurting. Only much later would I learn the truth.

In the other bed Kyle was sleeping with one leg over Josh's face while Justin was curled up over to the side. They looked like pretzels. Casey had the other bed all to himself.

I just smiled shaking my head as I made my way into the bathroom, then into the shower. How happy I felt! What a wonderful time we were having! I really loved these great kids of ours! My heart was full to overflowing with love for each of them! This was, truly, how being a granddad should feel!

After getting ready for the day, I quietly left the room to go get my morning coffee. I strolled up to the lobby where they had free coffee along with a continental breakfast. I was sorely disappointed that they didn't open till eight. These people up north sleep late!

Walking back to the van, I was thoroughly enjoying the brisk morning air. I drove through town to the first service station I came to and went inside to get myself my morning shot of caffeine. Like many places like this, it had a mini convenience store inside. A middle-aged man was barking orders at a young girl behind the counter who appeared to be new on the job.

After pouring my coffee I went to the counter where she rang it up. She looked like she was about 18 and she was absolutely dazzling—blonde hair with blue eyes wearing a name tag that said, Hanna, the same as our granddaughter. Wait till the boys see her!

Driving back through town, sipping my coffee, I could see that not many people were up yet. Before I knew it, I was back at the motel. It was nearly eight now, so I woke the boys. They each took a shower and brushed their teeth while I warmed the chocolate chip pancakes I made the day before and cooked some turkey sausage links in the microwave.

These guys ate every pancake as well as nearly two pounds of sausage. What appetites youths have...Especially boys! They would need all their energy before this day was over...and then some!

After getting into the van, I told them I had a surprise for them, then, I drove straight to Hanna's place. We all went inside to get drinks after I told them what to expect. They were all smiling as we left. Really big smiles! Girls are so wonderful—even better than baseball. Okay...it's a tossup!

This morning was off to a great start! Hanna received a unanimous rating of nine. She even got high marks for personality. What a compliment coming from these five. If she were only wearing a bikini I'm sure she would have received a perfect 10………..Aw shit!

Now we were ready to hit the road, Jack!

Within a minute, the highway began its gradual turn right that will follow Route 2, west, along the north shore of Lake Michigan to our first destination of Fayette Historical State Park. Grandma Lee and I first traveled there shortly after we were married. Her two girls and my three boys went with us. It was a bonding period. They were about the same age as our grandsons are now. The circle of life.

It would take about 90 minutes to get there, I informed everyone. Not to worry, though, as it is a lovely, peaceful, drive with the magnificent shoreline of Lake Michigan visible for much of our drive.

The boys marveled at the sandy beaches of this beautiful lake only a few miles outside of St. Ignes. This time of the morning the waves were gently caressing the shoreline. This is where they will swim on our way back to the motel if we don't find a better spot, farther up the road.

We had the radio tuned to a music station that was playing music of my liking, but not so much theirs. "Grandpa, turn it to 87.5," they pleaded. A combination of hip–hop, mixed with lyrics I could almost understand, instantly, pounded from the speakers. The beat was contagious, and I started seat dancing to the laughter of all the boys.

We were having a great time; the old lion and the young cubs—and the day was just beginning!

A Star is Born

To my utter amazement, Kyle, our prolific homerun hitter, (two grand slams, **over the fence**..... in **one** inning!) starts belting out every word to every song without missing a beat. I smiled broadly, not believing my ears. It seemed he knew every lyric to every song that was being played.

Casey asked, unbelievingly, "Kyle, do you know all the words to every love song!!!" Kyle just smiled broadly and kept right on bopping. We all cracked up!

I was still rocking to the beat as we traveled toward Garden Corners, where we would turn left toward Fayette. Ten minutes later, we came to the first of what would be many stops for road construction. It seemed to take forever before we saw cars coming down the only lane open for travel. There was an endless stream of them. When it was finally our turn to go, I found out why. The road work being done was for a mile of road, each time.

I had mixed feelings as the State of Michigan has the worst roads in the country. They were neglected for the entire eight years of our former Governor, Jennifer Granholm's term in office. Many were in such bad shape it was not only shameful, but they were downright dangerous to drive on, especially for motorcycles.

So, I was actually glad that this scenic highway was being repaired. Being honest, I would have preferred it be done when we were not traveling it, though.

Well, I thought, maybe they will be finished by the time we come back.

We kept on rocking and I kept on driving. Our energy level was high. A great start to a great day! The weather was perfect, too; hardly a cloud in a gorgeous, baby-blue sky.

Josh was doing a thing with his voice that absolutely drove Casey into hysterics. That in turn caused Joey to wonder, out loud, how Casey could think it was so funny, especially, after hearing Joshua do the same voice so many times.

In answer to Joey, Josh instantly, did the voice again and we all burst into laughter, right along with Casey. It was impossible not to. This boy simply had a knack for cracking you up!

All the great music and all the great chatter don't help much, though, when you just want to reach your destination and get out of this darn van. This ride was taking way too long.

I had been telling the boys that it would only be 30 minutes longer till we turned off to go to Fayette for well over an hour now. Somehow, I don't think they had a lot of faith in my estimates at the moment.

When I gave them the original estimate of a 90-minute drive, I forgot that I used to drive much faster than I do today. Of course I didn't take into account the ever-present construction stops either.

Finally, we did reach the turn off at Garden Corners and started the last few miles to the park.

Just a few miles away was the small burg of Garden. It had a saloon that looked as if it had a dress code, too. If you, unwittingly, walked in without a six-shooter they would give you one. I doubt they served my Merlot there.... I'd bet on moonshine and homemade beer, though! I'd have to be mighty thirsty to go in there. And much braver than I am.

Fayette Finally

It was just a few minutes more till we were in the parking lot, happily, getting out of our van. We walked down a few steps into the souvenir shop that housed a working model of the town when they were smelting iron ore. They started two years after the Civil war ended, in 1867.

All we had to do was press a button and a voice explained every detail of the process. As each detail was explained, a small section of the display would light up as it was being described. It was interesting, but we wanted to explore this place.

The six of us hurried down a long flight of concrete steps till we reached a large asphalt walkway that led to dirt walking paths. We could see several restored wooden buildings and a large, partially restored, stone structure all overlooking one of the most beautiful harbors, ever. It is called, Snail Harbor; part of the Lake Michigan shoreline that is known as Big Bay de Noc. The water is so clear here that people scuba dive, to explore the many artifacts that lie on the bottom. There is also a long docking area for pleasure boats that travel the Lake.

We walked by the twin blast furnaces that have not been used since 1891. We see a huge, brick, structure beside it about 40 feet away. It is in the shape of a tee-pee. I think it was used to make the charcoal for the twin blast furnaces to burn. Now, many of the faces of the bricks have fallen off, ravaged by the cold Michigan winters.

As one, the boys ran to it and immediately began to climb the 20 feet to its top. They all stopped about halfway up and I had them pose for me as I snapped a few pictures before they began their decent. Only Kyle and Justin were left on it, not able to find their footing back down.

I walked over to help Justin down first as Kyle was higher up. Kyle was hesitant to come down because he couldn't feel, or see, where to put his feet. While we all barked instructions he continued to climb even higher. Now he was in the danger zone.

If he lost his footing he could be hurt really bad, sliding against this rough brick surface to a fall ten feet below. He was on the narrow end of a cone so there was no way to jump down.

Two older ladies stood in the shadows, anxiously, watching as this drama unfolded. They were snapping a few pictures to record this accident that was about to happen.

I knew there was only way for this to end happily. I had to climb up several feet and reach up with one hand to take Kyle's feet, one by one, and place them in the nooks and guide him, step by step, safely down. If he fell now, his 140 pounds would land on my old body and who knows what would happen then. That would be a great picture for the ladies, but not so much so for Kyle and me.

It took only a few minutes to climb up and guide him safely down. As his feet touched the ground once more I was relieved...we were both alright. Justin cheered loudly for his grandpa, yelling, "Grandpa you did it! You rescued him!"

By golly that made me feel like a hero. I put my arm around his shoulder, gave him a little love squeeze and thanked him for his praise. It felt really good! He's such a great kid.

Climbing Everest

Next, I led my gang over to the beginning of a path that once led to the top of this sheer rock cliff. It was a scary sight to behold from the bottom. I remembered it not being as scary a climb as it now looked, though. Many years had passed since I first climbed it and erosion had been hard at work. I wasn't worried as we began our climb with absolute glee.

Boys, big and small, love this kind of adventure for some crazy reason. It's in our DNA.

The climb was not as easy as I remembered it. It began to be a challenge right from the start and only got worse as we climbed higher.

Finally, when we had a 4-foot chasm to cross, and if any of us fell now we would probably kill ourselves, I knew it was time to stop. This was much too dangerous so I called a halt and we carefully worked our way, straight down.

I was the last to descend so when my feet finally touched the huge rocks that lined the bottom my boy, Justin, once more marveled, "Grandpa you were the only one who kept his footing all the way down! You were the only one of us that didn't end up on his butt."

"Justin, that is because Grandpa grew up in the hills of West Virginia," I bragged…. "I'm used to this kind of thing."

It was a great compliment, I thought happily till I almost lost my balance on a huge, slanted boulder at the water's edge and nearly fell on my rear end! I was still slightly dizzy as I regained my footing and steadied my swirling brain.

My grandsons were all concerned as they each asked anxiously, "Grandpa, are you all right?"

I'm okay, I answered, just a little red faced…. Wow, that was close!

We stood on such massive boulders that had broken loose from the mountain, who knows how long ago, that it felt really special for each of us to be standing there now, witnesses to nature's sheer power.

Casey picked up a rock and we started a contest to see who could skip his rock the most times across this peaceful bay. My once strong throwing arm had left me long ago, and I was fortunate to throw a lucky one that skipped four times before sinking under the water. I think it won the day—although Casey threw one that was very close.

Shortly thereafter, we made our way back across to the other side. There was only one boat docked there today. It was a fine craft without being too showy. It was not huge but still large enough to navigate these waters, even in stormy weather. The people aboard seemed pleasant enough though somewhat preoccupied.

We walked past them and an older couple sitting nearby on a bench. Then we descended a small grade to a spot where timbers stood upright at the waters edge.

The shoreline here was completely covered with small rocks of every size and shape as well as many different colors. It is the same lovely spot where I once stood and took pictures of our children….. these boy's parents, many years ago.

Still, I remembered it so well as the memory, instantly, flooded my mind. It tugged at my heartstrings as I thought of my hopes for us as a family way back then when we first started our life's journey together and the future was so uncertain.

Now I am taking pictures of the very children who fill our own children's hearts with that special love that only a mother and father feel. What a precious moment I thought!

I said a silent prayer of thanks for this very special time and for all of God's blessings.

As we began to explore the little village, the three older boys went one way while Justin and Kyle walked with me; actually, going into the buildings to see how life was back then. This is an amazing piece of Michigan's, as well as our country's, history.

The structures each have documents that list its history. There are many original tools here that they used back then, but the most interesting thing to me were the names of the people—both men and women and where they came from...as well as their children's names; birthplaces; and their ages.

In some of the buildings there are handwritten documents. This was history in its truest form.

You will never find more exquisite handwriting anywhere.... I mean that! Our handwriting leaves something to be desired compared to our parents, but the handwriting of our children and our grandchildren is usually terrible; especially, in comparison to those who lived 150 years ago.

The flowing lines of their letters...the absolute level and precise size of their sentences, somehow, made me feel as if I lived back then and actually stood by, watching the author write it. I felt a kinship with him and a sorrow that he lived such a hard life.

We called the three older boys into one of the structures that housed some of the larger tools the men who lived here used. In it there was a huge picture of many of the workers posed in front of the twin blast furnaces.

One lone man stood high on the top. Joshua immediately said that would be him. Most of their faces were dirty from hard work and sweat. The poster said they worked 12-hour days, 7 days each week.

The pay seemed cheap, even for those days. Many had traveled from Bulgaria, Belgium, Ireland,

France, and Canada for a better life here in America. If this was a better life, I could only wonder what kind of life they left behind.

I hoped that our grandsons would realize just how blessed they were to be born in the age they were born in—as each of them had an expensive phone cradled in his pocket.

Folks who work that hard had to have some kind of entertainment, and these people did. They built a theatre with a small stage, and we could only imagine the joy they felt putting on the shows.

Today, my boys were the featured attraction as I snapped their pictures while they mugged for the camera...standing on this stage where these hard-working people stood, a century and a half before.

Big Springs

We had been here about 2 hours now, and it was time to move on. Our next stop was the one they would later say was their favorite to see.

The Indians called it Kitch-iti-kipi, which means Big Cold Water. They also called it, Mirror of Heaven, because of its emerald, green waters which are crystal clear. It's the limestone bottom that makes it look like that.

It is Michigan's largest natural spring. It is oval shaped, measuring 300 feet by 175 feet, and it's about 40 ft deep with water that is a constant 45 degrees. An amazing 10,000 gallons of pure, clean, water gushes from its limestone and sandy bottom, every minute.

In the 1920's, in nearby Manistique, a five and dime store owner by the name of John Bellaire, came upon it while exploring the area and immediately fell in love with it.

In 1926 he talked Frank Palms, owner of the Palms Book Land Company, to sell it to the State of Michigan, along with 90 acres of land for the unbelievable sum of $10.

That's an even better deal than we got Manhattan Island from the Indians for. Later, the State acquired another 210 acres, so the park now encompasses 300 acres.

As we drove into Palms Book State Park where it is located, we are surrounded by thick woods of mostly tall pines and cedar trees.

The boys were very happy that they only had a 30-minute drive to get here and so was I.

We walked down a paved pathway, through a wooded area, to the water's edge. There, a large wooden raft that would take us out on the water was being, hand cranked, back into the dock by other visitors.

The raft is attached to a thick, steel, cable that stretches across the pool to its docking area. It is propelled by one person, turning a large metal steering wheel, in the direction you want to travel. To go away from the dock, it is turned counter–clockwise—to return, it is turned clockwise.

The moment we got near the water, each boy's heart raced with excitement as they saw huge fish, clearly visible, swimming leisurely in the crystal-clear water.

There looked to be hundreds of them. They were a mixture of lake trout, brown trout, and brook trout, and they were all really big, all gliding slowly, seemingly, without a care in the world.

Gazing into the clear emerald water, they looked to be nearly 3 feet long, and somehow, they all looked to be about the same size.

These fish would probably be some of the best tasting, ever. Talk about organic; I can't imagine fish being so free of contaminants. All for naught, though, as there is no fishing allowed here.

Within minutes the raft had docked and the six of us, as well as a young man with two female companions, boarded...lucky guy!

I took control of the wheel and with moderate effort moved us, slowly, away from the dock. There would be no water skiing today!

We could see the bottom clearly, as it gradually got deeper and deeper. Carcasses of several dead fish lay peacefully, undisturbed, on the bottom.

There was no vegetation at all. We could see the sandy bottom, swirling, as the underground water forced its way upward, through the sand and into the large pool.

All the while, the fish were in no hurry as they continued their carefree swim.

At the deepest point I left the wheel and walked the few feet to the center observation hole. I reached into my pocket and removed a penny, then dropped it into the pool.

We watched its slow descent to the bottom, as it turned over and over and glided straight down. I was a little alarmed as several fish hurried over to taste it.

Each fish knew better, though, and the penny moved sideways for just a second, as they blew water out of their mouths to make it dance its lonely, silent, dance.

It landed softly on the bottom and sank immediately into the soft sand.

I took the wheel once more and moved us closer to the far side, before turning the wheel in the opposite direction, as we made our way, slowly, back to the dock.

After our fellow tourist left, I had five happy youngsters pose for a few pictures. One day these photos will refresh their memories—and for just a short moment in time, they will once more, be young and carefree...feeling the exuberance they feel, today.

I know their faces will soften into heart–felt smiles as they think back to this day and all the fun they had with each other. Just, maybe...their Papa will find a moment in their hearts, too.... I hope so.

Before we left, we went into the souvenir shop where they also had an ice cream stand. These guys were hungry by now and everyone wanted double dippers.

Back in the van, driving down the unfamiliar roads, I must have made a wrong turn at the first junction we came to. Fortunately, within 15 minutes or so, we were entering the town of Manistique from the back side.

Let's go Swimming!

Within a few more minutes we were back on Route 2, headed east. I guess, even, I couldn't get lost up here.

They all wanted to test the waters of Lake Michigan ASAP. Every spot we passed where we could pull over they pleaded for me to stop, no matter how rocky the shoreline was. Remembering the beautiful sandy beaches we passed on our way here, I kept delaying the moment, though.

They were having a good time with each other, so they weren't too demanding or impatient. I was thinking of how well our day had been so far.

I was pleased that they really liked both places we visited

today, and that they had had such a great time. With young men like these you never know.

We had been on the road about 30 minutes before we came upon our first construction delay. Because it was later in the day, traffic was even heavier, and the stops were even longer.

After the third one we came to, we all started to get a little impatient with the long waits. They wanted to swim, and I wanted to get to our room where I could relax for the first time today.

All this driving and walking was beginning to take its toll.

After what seemed like forever, we rounded a curve and stretched out in front of us was about a mile of sandy shoreline, with a long line of cars pulled off to the side of the road. People were scattered on the sand near the water, on beach towels, loungers, and folding chairs.

What a welcome sight! Finally, we had arrived!

They changed into their swim trunks in the van, trying, mightily, to hide their nakedness. Within seconds, they were scurrying out the doors, down a small grade, and onto the beach; then, into the blue, rolling, waves!

Smiling, I watched my Fab Five dive into the cold waters of Lake Michigan. My heart was mush by now. Their happiness was contagious. This trip was even better than I imagined it could possibly be.

Nothing could be this good...and it wouldn't be much longer before I learned that lesson...in Spades!

It was about four in the afternoon, and I hadn't eaten a thing, yet. I knew they were all hungry, too, so I began to put together the hamburgers I packed for us. I made the first one for myself while they swam.

Hungrily, I bit into my lukewarm burger. I couldn't believe how good it tasted. I must have been hungrier than I realized. That, and some potato chips, along with a little water to drink, and I felt almost human again.

After fixing five more burgers, I put them on the dashboard, so the sun coming through the windshield would warm them a little. I knew how hungry they had to be and wanted the burgers to taste their best.

Casey and Josh were the first two to leave the cold waters of Lake Michigan and come back to our van. As they started to get into the van, I noticed that their feet were heavily covered with sand, well above their ankles.

I called a halt to that, while they walked with me back down to the water's edge. I was carrying the plastic container the hamburger meat was in. It was covered with grease, so I washed it the best I could with sand and had the boys rinse it and fill it with water.

I had them sit down, with their legs out of the van, while I washed the sand from their feet, then, dried them with a towel.

After doing that, I handed them their plates with their hamburger and chips on it, along with a cold juice pouch to wash it down with.

After waiting another ten minutes, I walked back down to the water's edge, where much farther out, Joey, Justin, and Kyle, were still happily swimming. Waving my arms and yelling for them to come in, I could see that that wanted to enjoy this huge lake with its rolling waves a little longer.

I didn't rush them, as they slowly made their way back to the beach. After going through the same routine with their feet as with the other two, I told them where their burgers were.

Grandpa Loses It

Standing at the tailgate, putting things back together, once more, I watched as Kyle handed Joey his burger. It looked as if a great white shark had bitten into it, and I commented that he must have been really hungry to take such a huge bite out of it. He said, "Papa, I didn't do that." Justin piped up, instantly, saying, "Grandpa, Joshua did that! He took a big bite out of Kyle's and mine, too!"

I saw red! "Joshua, you f---head. Why would you do something like that? Do you think Joey wants to eat that after you already ate half of it?" Joey agreed that he didn't want it, so turning once more to Joshua, I said, "You might as well finish it, because nobody else will eat it now."

I learned later that Joshua stuffed it into his sock as soon as I got into the van and started to drive away. Of course, everyone gave him a big smile when he did. We used to call it "showing off" or "being a smart ass." Why did this kid have such a propensity for this kind of behavior?

He knew full well that Kyle, Justin, and Joey, would be upset by what he did. He knew they were hungry, too, just as he had been. He knows me, too, after being around me so much over his 13 years. He knew I would be greatly upset over this...so why would he still mutilate their hamburgers in spite of knowing how we would all feel?

Yet, it hurt that I got so angry with him. It was almost as if I was taken back in time to when my sons were small and I had to discipline them. It always hurt me more than it did them, and this felt the same.

We pulled into the parking lot of our motel about 20 minutes later. After fixing Joey another hamburger, I asked Josh to come out onto the balcony with me. The other boys were hurrying into their swim trunks to go look for Ms. Bikini.

After we sat down I began to talk to this young man, whom, I love so much and have such high hopes for. I started by saying that today could be a turning point in his life. I explained that I had a similar moment in my own life, when I was about the same age.

I related that my parents moved to a new neighborhood when I was in the 9th grade, so I decided I wanted a fresh start. I wanted to be a better person and to be friendlier to the kids I hung around with, as well as everyone else, too. I determined to limit my smart remarks and not make others a butt of my jokes. Also, not always be so ready to fight, either.

I related that Jewish boys accepted the responsibilities of manhood at age 13, when they have their Bar Mitzvah. That at that age they were considered smart enough, as well as old enough, to know the difference between right and wrong and to adjust their behavior accordingly.

Joshua sat and listened intently as I continued to speak. He is not a bad kid at all. I want, so much, for the best for him, as well as all the others, too. Don't all grandpas?

I told him that he needed a ten second delay in his brain, before he did this kind of thing. In those 10 seconds, he needs to think of the consequences of his actions; and if it would be hurtful to any other person, don't do it.

I asked how he thought his Grandma Lee felt when he talked back to her, as he often does—or just ignores what she is saying to him and continues to do whatever he wants, regardless, if it upsets her, or not. Then I asked him a direct question.

"Joshua, do you think that kind of behavior causes her to love you, more?" Looking guilty as charged, he shook his head no, as he, also, said the word out loud. "Then...why do it?" I asked.

I went on to say that it didn't matter if you were a great basketball player; if you made fun of others on your team, after the game was over, they would want little to do with you...but if you helped them and encouraged them to be their best, they would go to battle for you. Knowing his love for basketball and baseball, I could see this made an impression.

Finally, I finished, saying it was all up to him. Then I hugged him, kissed him on the cheek, and told him I loved him. I added that I hoped he would remember my words and act accordingly.

With a relieved smile on his face, he hurried into his swim trunks and headed for the pool and Ms. Bikini. I retrieved my lovely wine glass and poured the last of the bottle into it. Unfortunately for me, I drank an extra glass the day before and now was sipping the last of my sweet nectar. Man…. I wished right now, I had that 2nd glass.

Little did I know that I'd need more than one more glass of wine before this night was over!

The Hot Tub

I moved over to the bed nearest the door to watch the action. They were all gathered at the far end of the pool, not much more than 100 feet from where I sat on the bed. Delilah had Sampson and his cousins buzzing around her like bees around honey.

These two were much too interested in each other, as they stood side by side in the water... not, to find some way to be alone, before long.

This was the last evening they would see each other. I knew something was going to happen. It was almost like a soldier going off to war and he was spending the last hours with his girl. Something's got to give!

As I watched them, the memories of my own youth came flooding back. I was suddenly transported back to a front porch in W.Va., where I sat with a pretty girl who was visiting her aunt for a few days. It was the last day she would be there.

Somehow, she chose me out of all the guys in our neighborhood. We had a beautiful, star-filled sky, with just a sliver of a bright moon to serenade us, as we sat in her aunt's swing. It was a warm summer night, and we were so hot for each other we couldn't stand it.

The newness of holding a young woman in my arms, and the exquisite feeling of her soft mouth, seeking mine in a passion filled kiss, was almost more than

I could bear...yet I couldn't get enough.

We held each other for hours, with our bodies pressed softly together one minute; then, tightly clinging, the next. The feeling of her ample, yet soft breasts was driving me crazy. Few words were spoken, between the sweetest kisses a young man could ever taste.

When her aunt finally told her it was time to go inside, and we had one, last, passionate kiss, I knew this was the life for me. Thank God, I was born a man!
Hot diggity, dog diggity! This was so great! Who needs baseball, anyway!

It's a good thing I only had a short walk home. Our passion, without fulfillment, had done something magical to my testicles, and I could barely walk. Just my legs brushing against them brought such intense pain.

I walked as if I had been riding a horse all day long, with both legs spread widely apart, as I slowly made my way home.

It was the sweetest pain I've ever felt and was nothing compared to the fantastic memory. Thank you, you wonderful girl! Now it was my grandson's turn!

As I watched he and Delilah climbed out of the pool and walked side by side, toward the small room that housed the hot tub. I wanted to scream, "Don't go in there, Casey. That hot tub's dangerous!" as my wife and I had visited it several times, not so many years ago, and it always made us do naughty things. With their hormones raging like a wildfire, they didn't stand a chance in an evil hot tub like that.

Oops, too late, I thought, as they walked through the glass door and out of sight. Let the games begin!

With the lovers out of sight, I moved off the bed and started our dinner. This evening it was hot dogs, baked beans, and red skin potatoes. But I knew the boys could care less.

It wasn't long before Joshua came rushing through the door. "Grandpa! .... Casey and Delilah have been in the hot tub for 13 minutes! She's lying on top of him now, and they haven't stopped kissing!" Shockingly, to me, he added, "How disgusting!" Grabbing his phone to record this tryst, he hurried excitedly back out the door.

I thought...Joshua, if it was you doing what Casey's doing right now, you would not be saying that! Then, I asked myself a question.... Should I go in there and make them come out?

Hell, no! ...was my instant answer—that's her grandpa's job, not mine. Casey would never speak to me again, and I wouldn't blame him if he didn't. I just kept right on cooking and hoped grandpa would get there in time.

Only a few minutes passed before Joey, Kyle, and Justin, came in to report the same thing

Joshua had. They were all laughing and, absolutely, bursting with excitement, as they each snatched their phone and hurried back to take pictures through the glass door.

What a moment in time, I thought! These guys will never forget this! What a hero their cousin Casey is right now—He be da man!

Here come da Judge

Another ten minutes passed before I saw her grandfather walk past our door, heading for the pool. His was a stride with a purpose, not a leisurely walk.

The boys told me later that he knocked loudly on the door and ordered his granddaughter out of there. Just in the nick of time...... I hoped.

Casey followed, instantly. Great timing, I thought, as I was just putting their food on the table. I called them in to eat.

Has anyone ever heard five young guys, their ages, talking, after a scenario like that? I don't remember their words, but I can tell you right now, these guys were far beyond just being happy.... They were absolutely giddy!

Their naughty giggles; the excitement in their voices; all directed toward Cousin Casey, the new stud from Texas. He had, just cemented a lasting place in their hearts and in their memories as well. He was a bonafide hero!

"Aw Shit," I thought—This is what being a teenager is all about!

They ate quickly, then we watched as the young girl and her cousin sat against the glass wall, with their backs to us. They were the only ones in the pool area, and from their body language, the conversation seemed serious.

She was taking the brunt of the blame, while Casey did the manly thing and continued to hide like a rat in our room; unsure of just how much her grandpa had seen.

Joey and the other boys were trying to talk Casey into going back into the lions den; while he seemed content to watch the lovely lass from our window.

Another ten minutes passed before Joey led the other boys back to the pool area. Casey followed cautiously; still not sure what to expect.

Evidently grandpa was okay with the situation as long as he could see that nothing was going on. Good boy, Grandpa! Give him a hug, Grandma! A BIG ONE!

For the remainder of the evening the seven of them hung out around the pool; just being the young people they were. The young woman was clearly the center of attention, and who could blame her for loving it.

It's not every day that a girl has five good looking boys panting for her.

I sat on the balcony, thoroughly enjoying the view and the cool breeze coming off Lake Huron. I had promised the boys a pizza before bedtime, and it was now getting close to the time to order it.

Around 10 the pizza came, and I called our grandsons in to eat. The young girl and her cousin called it a night, too, and walked back to their room.

We watched the Tigers lose to Casey's Texas Rangers, and by that time it was almost 11:30. I had a big day planned for the kids tomorrow: seeing Castle Rock and then, the Soo locks in Sault St. Marie, about an hour's drive away.

We turned the lights out, and I once more stretched out in the tiny roll-away bed. It had been a great day, but I was still troubled, somewhat, because of being so angry at Joshua earlier in the day.

After thinking about it for a few minutes more, I was almost glad it happened. I knew I would not have had the talk with him if it didn't happen, and it was past time for a talk like that to take place.

I knew that long after the memory of my getting mad at him passed, he would remember the great advice he got from his grandfather. He couldn't go wrong if he followed it.

I closed my eyes and drifted immediately into a peaceful, well-earned, sleep. So far, so good! Considering the totality of it all, I was one contented grandfather. I could hardly wait for tomorrow!
father. I could hardly wait for tomorrow!

Knock, Knock, Who's There

Bam! Bam! Bam! Bam! Bam! Rang loudly in my ears, as I leaped from the bed in a panic. What the hell was going on! Was the place on fire! I turned on the lights and rushed to the door. The clock said 12:26. I had been asleep less than an hour.

Opening the door I saw Ms. Bikini's grandfather, also in a panic. "Are your grandsons in bed?" he asked. Rubbing my eyes and looking around the room I saw two empty beds. "No!" ... I answered unbelieving, as I was furiously pulling my pants on.

Hurrying past him, he asked, "What are you going to do?" Groggily and really pissed, I snapped, "I'm going to find them!" "Is one of your grandkids wearing a green shirt?" he asked me.

Really angry now, I snapped, "How the hell should I know! I don't know what color their shirts are!" What the hell did this guy think I was anyway—a damn fashion designer! I was definitely in a kill mode! Those little bastards!

I had done everything in my power to make certain they had the time of their lives, and this is the thanks I get, I thought, as my mind raced with where they could be…. I'll kill them!

We only walked 20 feet before he pointed to the room next door. The curtain was not completely covering the window and through the 4-inch space, there sat

Justin, sitting on the end of the bed, just chatting away, happy as can be, without a care in the world!

Pounding on the window, I yelled, "You better get your asses back into our room, right now!" Panic and raw fear instantly filled his face. He looked worse than I did when Grandma Lee caught me dancing with another woman, at a bar, years ago.

I hurried back into our room and out onto the balcony, as the five traitors climbed over the railing, scurrying quickly back into our room.

Here, I had been whipping myself all evening because of getting mad at Joshua, and they had been planning this for the whole day!!!

It's a wonder I didn't have a massive heart attack! To go from being awakened from a sound and peaceful sleep, to this, in just 60 seconds, was like watching a fighter jet take off.

My entire body could feel the G forces as I screamed every obscenity I could think of at them, even reaching back into my childhood in a tough coal mining camp in the hills of West Virginia; where people *really* knew how to cuss.

They were moving very fast as they passed me — getting to the far wall... as far from me as they could get, and still be in the same room! Just Joey stood by the bed nearest me...only because he wasn't fast enough to get to the wall with his co-conspirators.

Turning first to Casey, I angrily hurled, "Casey, I wish you had never come here! I'm sorry I tried to make this so special for you!" ……. Instantly, the angry words tore a hole in my heart, but, still, I said them.

Next, to Joey, I continued, "Joey your grandmother and I bust our asses for you, getting up at 5 in the morning, fixing you your favorite chocolate chip pancakes and bacon; then bringing them to you, every Tuesday and Friday, so you can have a hot breakfast before school; and this is the way you thank me….Sarcastically, I added, "Thanks a lot!"

I knew this was Casey's idea, yet I also knew Joey may have been able to stop it. His cousins all had great respect for him and if he had not gone along, maybe they wouldn't have, either. The others were just followers, so I placed little blame on them. In their places I would have done the same thing.

"I'm going back to sleep now and if any of you assholes leave this room after I do...your mother and father will come after you, because I promise you...you won't be riding home with me!" A minute passed before I added emphatically, "I'll never trust any of you, ever, again!"

As I tried to get back to sleep, I kept thinking how they had this planned, probably, the entire day. They had even entered a vacant motel room. Who knows what would have happened if the manager caught them.

But the overriding thought was that they had played me for a sucker. It didn't matter, all my effort.... as their cook, their chauffeur, their tour guide, even their maid—"we'll fool, old, senile, grandpa; Ha, Ha, Ha" ...rang loudly in my ears!

I was still plenty mad and very disappointed in these boys who have such a huge place in my heart...but I was also, so tired by then, that I had no problem drifting, almost instantly, back to sleep.

I don't think any of my wonderful grandsons went to sleep right away, though. Certainly not with visions of sugar plums dancing in their heads!

The Apology

I was awake and ready for the day by 6:30. Casey had gotten in bed with Joey sometime after I went to sleep. Thinking of it —it was kinda' funny, now...seeing four young men, lying, squeezed tightly together, side by side, shoulder to shoulder, in the bed farthest away from the danger zone —while only Joey was on the bed closest to me…...

That thought brought a smile to my face. What a five–some they were! My anger had disappeared sometime during the night, and now I was feeling the brunt of my angry words. It was not a good feeling to have. Why the heck did it always seem to hurt me most!

I was not going to let them off the hook so quickly though, as I loudly, demanded, "Get out of the bed…. Now! Get all your things together! We're going home!"

The five of them stumbled out of bed rubbing their eyes thinking, oh, no, not him again! They quickly gathered their things, and we carried the cooler out and headed home.

Showing them that there was some hope for the day, we stopped by Hanna's place while I gassed up, got my morning coffee, let them buy a drink and a snack, and have one last look at lovely Hanna.

Before crossing the bridge, we searched for a place that was open at that time of the morning that sold smoked, white fish; a request that Kyle's dad, Mark, had asked for. Unfortunately, every place was closed at this early hour.

As we started across the bridge, I began speaking. Joey started to speak at the same time. I could tell he wanted to say that he was sorry about the night before, but I asked him to wait.

"Boys," I began, "I'm sorry for calling you the names I did last night. I didn't mean it. I was really mad —but your grandpa is like a volcano —I blow my top and then it's over. I don't hold grudges... so I want to leave all the bad feelings up here—not take them back with us."

Turning to Casey, who was in the seat behind me, I continued, "Casey, I am most sorry for saying the things to you that I did. Of course, I'm happy you are here with us. I feel really bad for saying that I wished you hadn't come to Michigan...forgive me. It's just that I held you and Joey most responsible for what happened…. You know how much I love you."

Casey answered, graciously, letting me off the hook. "Grandpa we deserved everything you said to us. I accept all the responsibility for what happened, it wasn't Joey's fault. It's just that I wanted to be with her a little longer before we left."

I responded to him by saying, "Casey, if it were me in your place, and I had something that looked like her, hot for me; I probably would have done the same thing."

"When I was your age I used to go into our local movie theatre, looking for any girl sitting alone. When I found one, I'd sit beside her—even if she was the only person in her row and start making out...if she was willing. I got lucky a few times like that!

Being one of the boys, once, again; I related a story that is close to my heart, still. The girl who lived across from us with her mother, invited me over for some fun and games one night, when I was almost 13. Her mom was stepping out for the evening, and she was a well-developed 13-year-old herself.

She was dressed in a negligee with her top clearly visible. What a wonderful sight for a boy my tender age to see! We began by playing Jacks, but I couldn't take my eyes off her beautiful breasts—bouncing, up and down…up and down—so the game was over, almost, before it started.

Next, she took me by the hand and led me into her bedroom. The words that doomed the evening were, "If I get pregnant, you know you'll have to take care of me and the baby." Talk about dousing a roaring flame with ice cold water…that did it for me! I was opening that door before you could say, Da, Da!

She hurried after me pleading with me to stay, but no way was that going to happen! I thought…. How am I supposed to take care of a baby!!! Hell…mom and dad have to take care of me! Is she crazy! Why the hell did she have to say something like that for, anyway!

After I finished my story I turned to Joey, asking what he had wanted to say, earlier. Looking very solemn, he replied, "Just the things you said, Papa."

Looks like that boy will get all the chocolate chip pancakes he wants! I was back in love with the five of them. They were once again my "Fab Five!" They really were, five, fantastic, young men, and I was proud of every one of them.

With young men like these we have nothing to worry about. I am sure they will all leave big footprints before they leave this world. For me, who knows how much longer they will have me in their lives; only God. They had seen the best and the worst of their grandfather...all in just two days. I know I've left a lasting memory on each of them.

Boys need more than just their dads to associate manhood with. I was lucky to have my Uncle Harve. It was him that apologized and dad that got pissed. They work pretty good together.

When we began this trip, my hopes were that it would be a memory of a lifetime for each of them. Thanks to them taking matters into their own hands and sneaking off to be with the darling, Ms. Bikini, I am sure it will be.

I feel very fortunate to have been able to spend every minute I spent with these young men of ours. Their love for each other only grew stronger with their shared time together. I'm thankful that I was a small part of that.

But......... would I do it all over again--- You bet I would—in a heartbeat! The next time, though, I'm bringing five pairs of handcuffs with me and I'm cuffing each one to their bed at night!

No girls in bikinis either!!!! Okay... well, maybe.... We'll see!

Epilogue

Veteran criminals make mistakes, sometimes, that eventually get them caught. Amateur criminals *always* do. Usually, it's their mouths that prove to be their downfall.

They so love their criminal acts, and actually getting away with it, that they can't help bragging to each other and to others about how smart they are.

The Trip has its own element of this phenomenon.

Smart phones and computers have given criminals the ultimate bragging tools. Facebook and You Tube are notorious. I'm on Facebook, myself. Casey and Joey are, too. Too bad for them!

It's come to my attention, from the use of these tools—that Casey and Joey are laughing their heads off these days, because they fooled their grandpa…. Big-time!

Would you believe that they actually sneaked out of our room the night before too and went down to the beach with you know who…. and never got caught???? No…. I didn't, either, but they did!

All but Kyle, who was too tired, like I was, to wake up when they tried to get him out of bed that very first night. He sure didn't miss all the fun the next night, though! Now that explains a lot.

Joshua asking me to stop and get him some Visine for his red eyes the next morning, that I thought was because of the chlorine in the swimming pool. How could I have known it was because he had barely any sleep?

Then, there was my surprise, seeing Joey lying on the floor the next morning. Now, I realize that was because Casey was dreaming of Delilah and probably reaching for Joey. A hard floor is a great choice in that situation.

So, what am I to think? That they don't love and respect me…. I know they do. But hey, wait a minute…. I know! How about Getting even!

Yes, I think this grandfather has to show this "Fab Five" that the old and the young, both, can play this game. When we go next year, God willing, I think I'll have a few tricks up my sleeve, even if I don't have a sleeve on.

Gee-whiz ...I'm the cook, ain't I?? Now what can I put in those pancakes to make them absolutely perfect for me? I'd be surprised if any of these boys will get more than 10 feet from a toilet the entire time we're there...unless, of course, they are swimming in Lake Michigan!

I have a feeling they'll be doing a lot of that! I'll pack some Preparation H, too— just in case.... King Size!!! They are all going to need it! We'll see what tricks they feel like playing on their old granddad then!

Hey... I bet I won't even have to worry about girls in bikinis either. Well....... perhaps that's asking a bit too much to ask for these five!

Ready for the boat trip to Mackinaw Island

Right to Left: Casey, Kyle, Joey D, Joshua,
and Justin in front

Crossing over to Mackinaw

Right to Left: Joshua, Casey, and Joey

Justin and Kyle ready to roll!

Docking at Mackinaw

Kyle, Casey, Joey, Joshua and Justin in front

The Carriage for the Grand Hotel

Casey, Joshua, Joey, Kyle and Justin

Relaxing at the Grand

Kyle, Justin, Joey, Joshua, and Casey

Joey the Artist

The Grand Dame of Mackinaw"

Kyle and Joshua

Having fun in the Parlor

Kyle, Justin, Joshua, Casey, Joey standing

Connoisseurs of the Arts

Joey, Kyle, Justin, Joshua, and Casey

The shores of Mackinaw

Justin, Casey, Kyle, Joey, Joshua

Eating our fudge, ummm, good!!!

Justin, Kyle, Joshua, Joey, Casey

Fayette Historic Village

The boarding house

Climbing the brick furnace at Fayette

Casey, Justin, Kyle, Joey, Joshua

Going swimming in Lake Huron

Snail Harbor at Fayette

Joshua, Casey, Kyle, Grandpa, and Joey

The Raft at Big Springs

Joey, Casey, Joshua, Kyle, and Justin in front

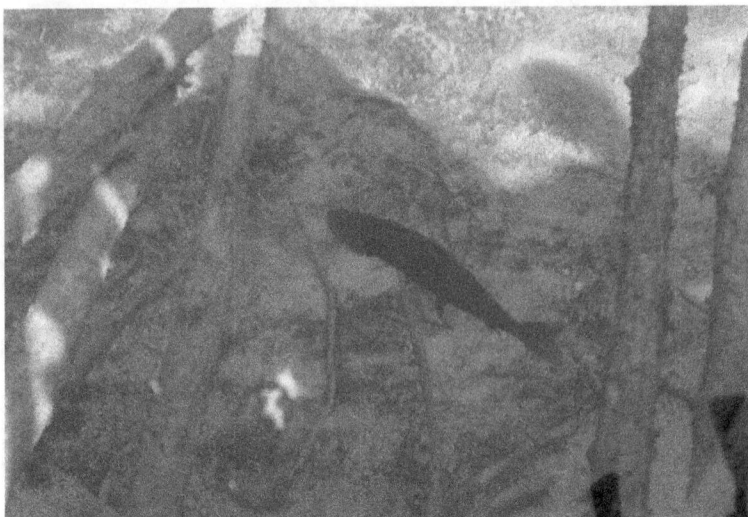

Lake trout at Kitch-iti-kipi

Lake trout at Kitch-iti-kipi

Kitch-iti-Kipi

Joshua, Papa, Casey, Kyle and Justin

Swimming in Lake Huron

Beach on Lake Michigan

Swimming in Lake Michigan

Where's Ms. Bikini

Casey, Justin, Joshua, Kyle, and Joey

Grand Hotel on Mackinaw

Tree of Life

Justin, Joshua, Casey, Kyle and Joey

About the Author

Doug graduated from Logan High School in Logan, W.Va., in 1960. His education at Logan High School in 1960 is the equivalent of a master's from Harvard or Yale in 2012, so he doesn't feel in the least bit deprived.

Although Doug failed to garner any academic awards, there was a general consensus among his teachers, that he had exceeded all expectations— by even graduating.

He pursued a career with GM, working on the assembly line as a spot–welder, building the soon to be defunct, Corvair, from May of 1961, till November of 1967. Most credit Ralph Nader with its failure, but those in the know place most of the blame on Doug.

Doug gave up that promising career to manage a Famous Fried Chicken carry-out for a very short period of time …less than one year. After nearly burning the place down one afternoon, he decided frying chicken was not good for him or for fried chicken lovers either.

Not easily discouraged, he began a career in the insurance field, where he is still employed and still working, at age 70.

Today, he manages (not too well) the Marcum Insurance Agency in Ypsilanti, Michigan. His wife, Lee, works with him and is probably the only reason they are still in business. That's what she says, anyway. A lot of their friends say the same thing, so okay, it's unanimous.

Since Doug's not exactly shined in any of his endeavors so far....

Thanks to his grandkids, he's decided to try his hand at writing. Any support at this stage of his life is greatly appreciated...The poor sap could really use a break about now... No kidding!